African Empires

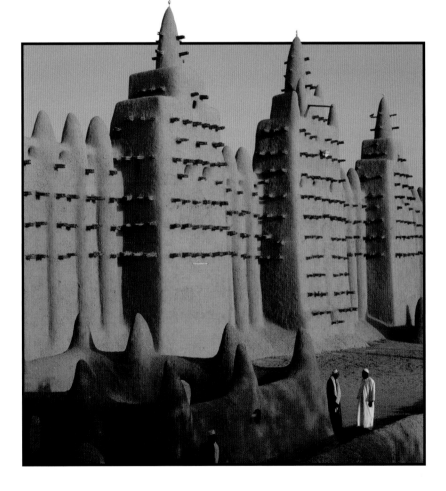

Dan Lyndon

FRANKLIN WATTS
LONDON•SYDNEY

This edition 2014
Franklin Watts
338 Euston Road
London NW1 3BH

Franklin Watts Australia
Level 17/207 Kent Street
Sydney NSW 2000

Series editor: Adrian Cole
Art director: Jonathan Hair
Design: Stephen Prosser
Picture research: Diana Morris

Dan Lyndon would like to thank the following people for their support in writing this book; The Black and Asian Studies Association (BASA), Marika Sherwood, Arthur Torrington, Joanna Cohen and Joanna Caroussis. Thanks also to the Lyndon, Robinson, Cohen and Childs families.

This series is dedicated to the memory of Kodjo Yenga.

Acknowledgements:
AKG Images: 34, 37br. Bonsai/Shutterstock: endpapers, 28. Borderlands/Alamy: 31b. British Library London/HIP/Topfoto: 30t. Jan Bruder/Shutterstock: 31t. Margarete Büsing/Ägyptisches Museum und Papyrussammlung, SMB/BPK: 14c. Archives Charmet/Bibliothèque Nationale Paris/BAL: 11t. Orne Christensen/Corbis: front cover r, back cover l. Mary Evans PL: 11b, 23tl, 32cr. Steffen Foester/istockphoto: 17t. Werner Forman Archive: 12, 13t, 17b, 21bl, 33br. Fourouklas/Shutterstock: 36. Paul Garland : 15b. Granger Collection/Topfoto: front cover l & b/g, back cover b/g, 6, 18, 22, 23. Maria Gropas/© UNESCO.All Rights Reserved: 13b. Gavin Hellier/Alamy: 5, 21tr. Colin Hoskins/Sylvia Cordaiy Pl/Alamy: 33t. Interfoto/Alamy: 8. Kharbine-Tapabor/PhotoBoistesselin/The Art Archive: 20t. Dusty Kline/Shutterstock: 36bl. Walter Knirr/Afripics/PD: 32cl. Lakis/Shutterstock: 33. Craig Lovell/Eagle Visions Photography/Alamy: 35br. Ricardo Miguel/Shutterstock: 10. Museo Arqueologico Nacional, Madrid, Spain / Photo © AISA/BAL: 19cr. Museu Nacional d'Art de Catalunya Barcelona/AISA/BAL: 23tr. National Anthropological Archives,©1999-2009 Smithsonian Institution. All Rights Reserved: 39t. National Army Museum London/BAL: 39b. National Maritime Museum London: 30b. Alfredo dagli Orti/Naval Museum Genoa/The Art Archive: 36tr. Gianni dagli Orti/Navy Historical Service Vincennes/The Art Archive: 28c, 29, 37tl. Ostill/Shutterstock: 14. Jenny Pate/Robert Harding Worldwide: 27br. Private Collection/Boltin PL/BAL: 16t. Private Collection/Stapleton Collection/BAL: 38. Royal Geographic Society London: 35t. James L Stansfield/National Geographic/Getty Images: 26-27. © UNESCO. All Rights Reserved: 24. University of Chicago, All Rights Reserved : 15t. World History Archive/Topfoto: 19bl. Ariadne van Zandbergen/Africa Image Library/PD: 25bl, 25br. Ariadne van Zandbergen/Afripics/PD: 19br.

Every attempt has been made to clear copyright. Should there be any inadvertent omission please apply to the publisher for rectification.

A CIP catalogue record for this book is available from the British Library.
Dewey number: 960
pb ISBN: 978 1 4451 3439 0
Library ebook: 978 1 4451 1516 0

Printed in China

Franklin Watts is a division of Hachette Children's Books, an Hachette UK company.
www.hachette.co.uk

Contents

Introduction

There is a famous African proverb that says "until the Lion has a historian of its own, tales of hunting will always be about the hunter". It means that, until recently, the history of Africa (the Lion) was not written by African historians. Instead, it was written by outsiders. Much of ancient African history was in fact recorded through oral traditions.

The Lion's tale

Our understanding of Africa was based on the tales and writing of outsiders; Greeks and Romans wrote about the ancient Egyptians; Islamic scholars followed the trade routes across the Sahara; and European missionaries wrote about the need to 'civilise' African people. Today, however, the Lion does have its own historian, and the story of Africa can be told in a way that speaks proudly of the great civilisations, powerful leaders, wealthy trade routes and natural resources of Africa. It also tells us that the peoples of Africa created strong communities with lasting traditions and cultures, and has a great history that is now being shared.

▲ Routes across the Sahara linked African communities and allowed them to trade. Later, the same routes were used by 'explorers', such as the one shown in this picture (dated 1853) travelling towards the great city of Timbuktu.

Oral history

One of the difficulties that African historians have had to overcome is the lack of written sources that are available. This is largely due to the fact that there is a strong tradition of oral history in Africa, with the past being handed down through stories and songs. However, this is still a very useful way of learning about African history, and in combination with the findings from archaeology, anthropology (the study of human beings), art history and the written sources that are available, a greater understanding has been achieved.

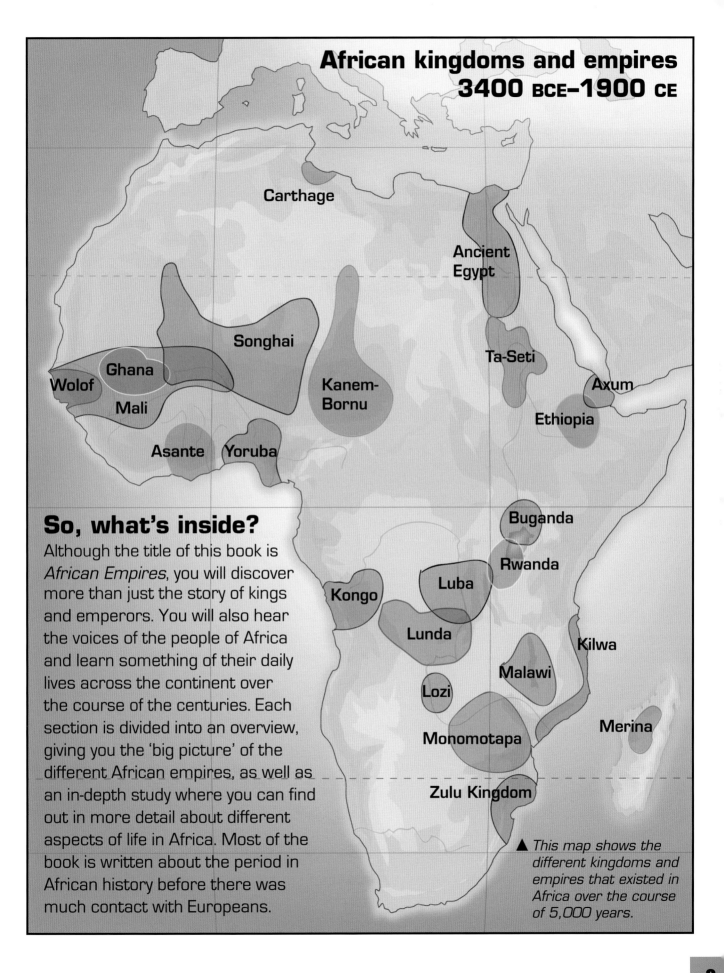

African kingdoms and empires 3400 BCE–1900 CE

Carthage

Ancient Egypt

Songhai

Ghana

Wolof

Mali

Ta-Seti

Axum

Kanem-Bornu

Ethiopia

Asante   Yoruba

Buganda

Rwanda

Kongo

Luba

Lunda

Kilwa

Malawi

Lozi

Merina

Monomotapa

Zulu Kingdom

So, what's inside?

Although the title of this book is *African Empires*, you will discover more than just the story of kings and emperors. You will also hear the voices of the people of Africa and learn something of their daily lives across the continent over the course of the centuries. Each section is divided into an overview, giving you the 'big picture' of the different African empires, as well as an in-depth study where you can find out in more detail about different aspects of life in Africa. Most of the book is written about the period in African history before there was much contact with Europeans.

▲ This map shows the different kingdoms and empires that existed in Africa over the course of 5,000 years.

African empires

The history of the African continent covers thousands of years, thousands of kilometres and millions of peoples speaking hundreds of languages. There are countless stories, dances, poems and songs. They tell the history of the great ancient civilisations, such as the Egyptians; the powerful kingdoms in West Africa of Mali and Songhai; the trading cities of Timbuktu and Gao; and enormous structures, such as the pyramids and Great Zimbabwe.

Trade and Empire

From the earliest times, people have traded with each other to provide for themselves and their communities. In Africa, this trade started with the exchange of raw materials that were found in parts of the continent. Records from c.1100 BCE show that trading in salt (used to preserve food) and metal (used in farming, hunting and bartering) was especially important. Trade routes opened up across the vast Sahara desert, linking the Muslim-Arab north with the sub-Saharan African communities further south, and even connecting with routes to India. This in turn led to the growth of different African empires, each competing to take control of the valuable trading routes. From the 15th century, as Europeans arrived on the coasts of Africa, stronger trade routes were opened up

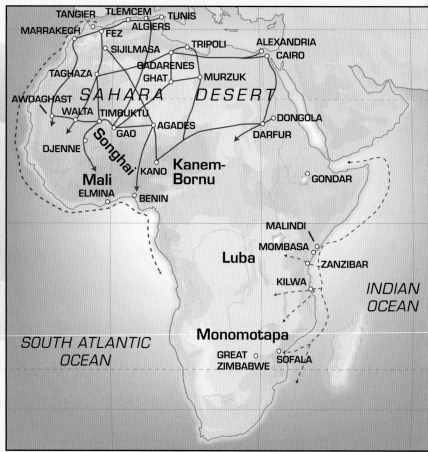

▲ This map shows the network of trade routes that existed across northern Africa in the 16th century.

with Europe, India and the Far East. While much of this trade was in gold, ivory, salt, pepper and other spices, the trade in human beings (slaves) also dramatically increased.

Religion and Empire

Christianity in Africa can be traced back over 2,000 years, and was matched later by the spread of Islam, particularly in north Africa in the 7th century. Religious influences were both positive and negative. Islamic scholars flocked to the great cities, such as Timbuktu in Mali, and set up important centres of learning. Christian missionaries from Europe set up schools which educated thousands. But both Muslims and Christians took active roles in the African slave trade. African emperors such as Mansa Musa, who ruled over the Empire of Mali from 1312 to 1337, were so strongly influenced by religion that they spent all their wealth following their beliefs. Others used religion to get support for their governments and maintain good trading relationships. Priests were even used to recruit soldiers for a country's army.

▲ This coloured ink picture from around the 12th century shows Islamic leaders at a meeting – probably in Baghdad (now part of modern day Iraq).

▼ The King of Kongo welcomes missionaries from Portugal in 1491. The king, formerly called Nzinga Mbemba, converted to Christianity and was renamed Afonso I.

Ta-Seti and ancient Egypt

What do you think about when you hear the words 'ancient Egypt'? Probably the pyramids and the pharaohs. I wonder if you knew that some of these came from a time before the ancient Egyptians?

The Kingdom of Ta-Seti, meaning 'the land of the bow', became established around 300 years before the First Dynasty of ancient Egypt formed in 3000 BCE (see pages 14–15). Archaeologists have discovered that the writing of ancient Egypt – the hieroglyphics – may well have originated from Ta-Seti. It has been argued that the people of Ta-Seti, sometimes called Nubians, provided the basis of Egyptian civilisation.

▶ *It is believed by some people that the origin of Egyptian hieroglyphics, like these, was in fact the Kingdom of Ta-Seti, which thrived in the Upper Nile valley. This area now forms part of Egypt and Sudan.*

The Egyptian Empire

The end of Ta-Seti marked the beginning of the first Egyptian Empire under the Pharaoh Narmer. (Pharaoh was the name given to the political and religious leader of Egypt, much like a king or emperor.) Narmer joined together the lands of the Upper and Lower Nile. As Egypt became wealthier, based on the rich farmlands around the Nile, trade increased and Egyptian cities grew. This was the start of the Golden Age of Egyptian history with the building of the pyramids, the development of the first calendar, the beginning of mathematics and the wide use of hieroglyphics.

Did you know?

The Upper Nile refers to the land in the south closer to modern day Sudan, whereas the Lower Nile refers to the land in the north in modern day Egypt. This is because it is in relation to the River Nile which flows to the north and ends up in the Mediterranean Sea.

Everyday life in ancient Egypt

Although Egypt was mainly an agricultural society, with farmers growing staple crops such as wheat, there were also large cities, towns and ports along the River Nile. Egyptian society ranged from high-ranking government officials to doctors and teachers, down to servants and slaves. Women were allowed to own property and run businesses, and there were also women pharaohs, such as Queen Nefertiti. Some things still common today were developed by the Egyptians, including make-up, shaving, using dyes to colour material, and wearing sandals and wigs.

▲ This image carved c. 1352–1336 BCE, shows Nefertiti (above left) kissing her daughter.

▼ These pyramids, built c. 900 BCE, are at Gebel Barkal in an area at the heart of the Kingdom of Ta-Seti. The fact that they are still standing today is evidence of the high-quality of work that existed at the time.

The Kingdom of Ta-Seti

IN DEPTH

In 1960, the Aswan Dam was built in Egypt to supply the country with hydroelectricity. However, this meant that some land had to be flooded, and the decision was made to build the dam over an area named Nubia. Today, evidence of people living in that area from at least 3800 BCE – people of the ancient Kingdom of Ta-Seti – lies at the bottom of the Aswan Reservoir.

An amazing discovery

In 1964, an archaeologist called Keith Seele was working in an area of Nubia called Qustul, when he discovered a huge cemetery containing 33 tombs; 12 of them were so large and impressive that he immediately thought that they must have been royal tombs, just like the ones from ancient Egypt. However, what was so interesting about them was their dates of origin, approximately 3800–3300 BCE. This meant that they came from before the First Dynasty of ancient Egypt.

Amazing finds

Seele and his team went on to excavate the tombs and found many different types of artefacts. There were over a thousand painted pots as well as gold jewellery, bottles, flasks, bowls and storage jars. There were also markings on some of the artefacts which were in hieroglyphics. This was an amazing discovery, because until that point it was thought that the ancient Egyptians were the first people to use hieroglyphs.

▲ This is just one example of the stunning gold jewellery found at Qustul.

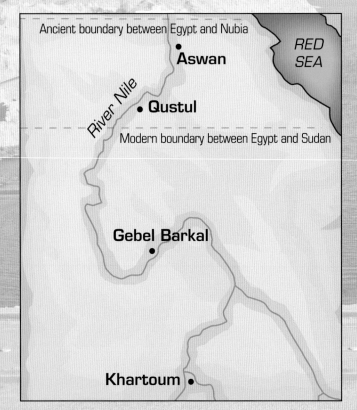

Ancient boundary between Egypt and Nubia

RED SEA

• Aswan

River Nile

• Qustul

Modern boundary between Egypt and Sudan

Gebel Barkal

Khartoum •

▲ This map shows the full extent of the Kingdom of Ta-Seti, and the city of Gebel Barkal.

The incense burner

One of the most fascinating objects to be discovered was a small incense burner (right), which was covered in pictures carved into its side. These images showed three ships sailing towards a royal palace. On one of the ships was a lion, on another ship was a prisoner being held by a guard and alongside these were images of a crown and a falcon: a royal bird in Egyptian culture. Did they suggest that the people of Ta-Seti worshipped a king? If so, it would seem that the ancient Egyptians got some of their ideas from Ta-Seti, and that perhaps later the two cultures overlapped in history. This argument is reinforced by other evidence from the area, which suggests that there were also pyramids built in Ta-Seti. So why is this important? Well, some people in the past argued that the ancient Egyptians were not part of 'Black Africa', that they

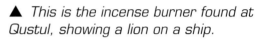

▲ *This is the incense burner found at Qustul, showing a lion on a ship.*

were instead closer to 'civilised' white Europeans. However these discoveries show that Black Africans were a significant influence on ancient Egypt.

▼ *This temple from Nubia was moved in the 1960s before the land was flooded by the Aswan Reservoir. It was given to the Netherlands for its help during the excavation.*

Ancient Ghana

Just as the Egyptian Empire was based on a strong agricultural and trading society, the West African empires developed along similar lines. The earliest records date back to 1100 BCE, and reveal the growth of large villages with stone buildings in the area known as Wagadu. By 300 CE, the ruler of the area was known as the 'Ghana', and that is why this part of West Africa became known as the Kingdom of Ghana.

▼ *This map shows the area that became the Empire of Ghana, and the central influence of the city of Kumbi Saleh. The red arrows show trade routes.*

▲ *This is a gold belt mask from Ghana. Gold played a central part in Ghanaian life, and many of its people were skilled metalworkers.*

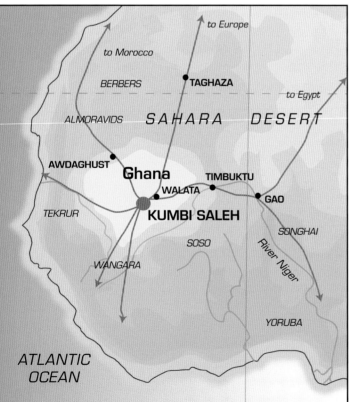

'The Land of Gold'

One of the most important reasons why Ghana grew in size to become an empire, taking over land both to the east and the west, was because of the amount of gold found there. The gold mines were very well concealed and as a result were well protected from attack. There was also a significant trade in salt, pepper, kola nuts, ground nuts and maize. The trade routes went north across the Sahara desert, and goods were often exported to Europe.

Did you know?

There are stories about the gold in Ghana that are so amazing that they are hard for us to believe today. The evidence suggests that the King of Ghana was one of the richest men in the world at the time. All of the gold nuggets that were dug up were taken to the king and exchanged for gold dust. One of the gold nuggets was so big, it is believed the king could tie his horse to it!

▲ *A large nugget of gold. The gold trade helped Ghana to establish itself as a wealthy empire.*

Emperor Tenkamenin

The most powerful ruler of Ghana was Tenkamenin, who ruled during the 11th century. He built an army of over 200,000 men, including 40,000 archers, and increased the size of his empire through a series of wars with local tribes. His capital, Kumbi Saleh, became one of the most important cities in West Africa (see pages 18–19). One of the greatest challenges Tenkamenin faced was against Muslim warriors coming from the north who declared a Holy War (jihad) against Ghana in 1076. Although the Muslims were eventually defeated, the Empire of Ghana had been so weakened that less than 150 years later it had been completely taken over by the Muslim rulers of Mali.

▶ *A terracotta figure, Mali c. 13th century. Rulers from Mali were attracted by the wealth of the Empire of Ghana and are believed to have invaded.*

What was life like in Kumbi Saleh?

IN DEPTH

My name is Abu Ubaid Al-Bakri and I want to tell you about the great city of Kumbi Saleh in ancient Ghana. Although I didn't visit Kumbi Saleh myself, I did hear from lots of people who had been there, and wrote *The Book of Routes and Kingdoms* in 1067, based on their stories.

▲ *This illustration shows part of a great walled city similar to Kumbi Saleh.*

"When I arrived at Kumbi Saleh, I was surprised to find that it was actually two cities, divided by a river. On one side was the royal city where the King lived with his court, and on the other the city of merchants and traders who were becoming rich from the 'Land of Gold'.

I first visited the court of Emperor Tenkamenin, and I was very impressed by what I saw. His Highness was seated in his royal pavilion, wearing necklaces and bracelets and a turban of fine cotton. He was surrounded by guards who were holding shields and swords made from gold, and at his right hand were the sons of the princes of his empire. At his feet were his chief ministers and advisors. Even the animals were beautifully decorated, with the horses and dogs wearing collars of gold and silver.

Al-Bakri

Abu Ubaid Al-Bakri (1014–1094) was born in Huelva, Spain, and was well known for his writings about Europe, Arabia and North Africa. This was despite the fact that he never once left Spain! Instead, he relied on information that he got from other travellers. His most famous work, *The Book of Routes and Kingdoms*, is an important source of information about the people, cultures, history, cities and climates of different countries around the world at that time.

When I left the court, I crossed the river to visit some of the businessmen who lived in Kumbi Saleh. I walked through the palm trees and henna plantations, until I came across a huge market where many different goods were being traded. I was fortunate enough to have some cowrie shells with me, which I exchanged for some kola nuts. I saw enormous bags of salt being loaded onto the camels for the trip north across the Sahara. I will have to make sure I have enough gold dinars to pay the export tax!

I also visited the great mosque of Kumbi Saleh. When I arrived I was in time for morning prayers, and there were thousands of worshippers. It was a shame that many of the people of Ghana still stick to their old religions, worshipping many gods and spirits.

Most of the people were living in mud huts but I did see some other domed buildings, and there was a large public square with buildings two storeys high. It was such a busy, bustling place. I believe that there are now something like 25,000 people living in Kumbi Saleh."

Items used in Ghana

Cowrie shells were used as currency in West Africa. They were originally from the islands of the Maldives in the Indian Ocean, and were brought to Africa by Muslim traders.

Gold dinars were coins used by Muslim traders. They get their name from an old Roman coin: the denarius. A dinar weighs 4.25 grams of solid gold.

Kola nuts have a bitter taste and people would chew them for their caffeine. They were used across West Africa for ceremonial purposes.

The Empire of Mali

OVERVIEW

Around 1200 CE, the decline of Ghana was followed by the rise of the Mali Empire, led by a great warrior king called Sundiata Keita (meaning 'the hungry lion'). Keita won a famous victory at the Battle of Kisine in 1235 CE, and at the age of 18 became the Mansa, or Emperor, of Mali. Stories tell of his great bravery and leadership; 'The lightning that flashes across the sky is slower, the thunderbolts less frightening and floodwaters less surprising (than Sundiata Keita)'. Over the next 200 years, Mali spread over 700,000 square kilometres (an area bigger than western Europe), and included more than 400 cities.

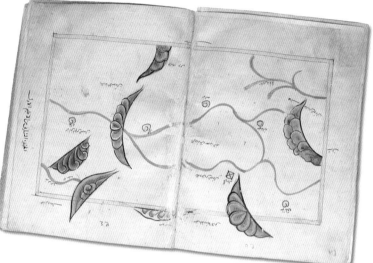

▲ This 12th-century map shows land which later became part of the Mali Empire. It shows mountains, with rivers in green and towns in yellow. [The map has been rotated to north, so the Arabic text is not displayed correctly.]

Protecting trade

Mali's wealth was based on the trade routes that had existed in Ghana. These included three enormous goldfields, which produced nearly half of all the gold in the world at the time. Salt, copper and slaves were traded throughout the Empire. In order to protect this trade, the Emperor had a full-time army of 100,000 men and 10,000 cavalry. The soldiers were trained to use a bow and poisoned arrows, a stabbing spear called a *tamba*, and used animal hides for their shields. The horses even wore chainmail to protect them.

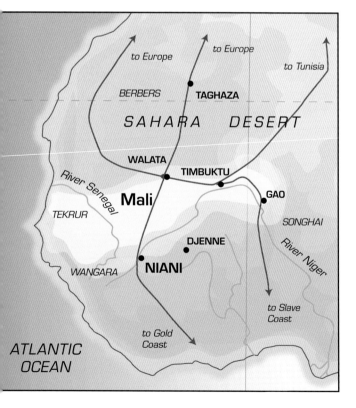

▲ The Mali Empire stretched from the River Senegal in the west to the River Niger in the east.

There is evidence to suggest that explorers from Mali discovered South America nearly 200 years before Columbus. According to this research, in 1311 the Emperor of Mali, Mansa Abubakari II, sent two voyages across the Atlantic Ocean. In Panama, where they may have landed, there are still places today called Mandinga Bay and Mandinga Town. The Mandinga were one of the tribes from Mali.

▲ *Djenne Mosque at Timbuktu still stands today. It was built by Mansa Musa in c.1326.*

▼ *Many people believe that the colossal heads from the Olmec culture in South America (one is shown here) are evidence that African people landed there before Columbus in 1492.*

Mansa Musa

One of the most famous emperors of Mali was Mansa Musa, who reigned from 1312 until 1337 (see pages 22–23). He made Mali even wealthier by capturing the cities of Gao and Timbuktu. By this time most of Mali's people were Muslims, and there were many mosques built during Mansa Musa's reign. However, parts of the Empire were not happy about having Islam as their religion, particularly in the Songhai region. After the death of Mansa Musa, there were a series of terrible droughts and these, combined with invasions from Songhai in the east, brought about the end of the Mali Empire.

Mansa Musa and the pilgrimage to Mecca

IN DEPTH

This is an imaginary interview with Mansa Musa, who was the Emperor of Mali from 1312 to 1337. In this interview, he is talking about his pilgrimage to Mecca in 1324, a journey that took nearly two years.

SCHOLAR: Good evening Your Majesty. How are you today?

MANSA MUSA: I am well, Allah be praised.

SCHOLAR: I believe that you have just returned from the Hajj to Mecca. How long did your pilgrimage take?

MANSA MUSA: I left Niani, my capital in 1324 and now, two years later, I have finally returned to my people.

SCHOLAR: Wow, that is a major expedition. How were you able to keep yourself in the manner that you are accustomed to?

MANSA MUSA: Well, obviously most of the members of my court came with me, and we travelled with 60,000 servants and 100 camels.

SCHOLAR: I understand that you spent some time in Egypt before you got to Arabia – what did you get up to there?

Did you know?

There were many languages spoken in the Mali Empire, although the name 'Mali' comes from the language of the Malinke tribe. Arabic was introduced to Mali by Arab traders who used the trade routes across the Sahara desert. Mansa Musa would have spoken Arabic, particularly as the Qur'an (the Islamic holy book) was written in Arabic.

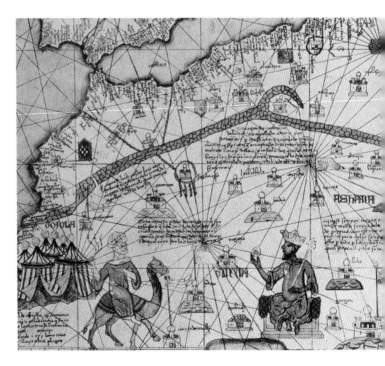

▲ This Spanish map from 1375 shows Mansa Musa (bottom right) seated on his throne.

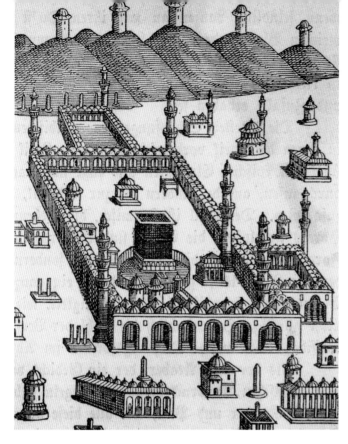

▲ A 15th-century illustration of the Masjid al-Haram Mosque in Mecca, which Mansa Musa would have visited on the Hajj.

MANSA MUSA: It was an important part of my Muslim beliefs to be generous to my Egyptian brothers and sisters, so every Friday at evening prayers I would give them gifts of gold.

SCHOLAR: Have you any idea how much you spent?

MANSA MUSA: My treasurer tells me that we left Mali with 24,000 pounds of gold [which in today's money is about three million pounds worth]. We returned with nothing. However, there were many mosques built with our gold. The problem was that I spent so much money that the value of the Egyptian gold market has slumped because there is so much gold available.

SCHOLAR: How did you get home in the end?

▶ This gold coin is from the 13th century, and is an example of the beautiful Islamic coins produced across an area covering Spain and Afghanistan.

MANSA MUSA: In fact, I had to borrow money from an Egyptian merchant to make sure that I could get back to Mali.

SCHOLAR: Did you bring anything back from your travels?

MANSA MUSA: Indeed, I bought some Turkish and Ethiopian slave girls, some singing girls and beautiful garments and cloth.

SCHOLAR: I understand that you also brought back with you some important scholars and architects from Egypt.

MANSA MUSA: That is correct. I want them to help me build some madrassas (Islamic schools) in Timbuktu. We will have the best schools and libraries in the whole of Africa. I want Timbuktu to be famous for the teaching of Islam around the world.

SCHOLAR: Many thanks, Your Majesty.

MANSA MUSA: My pleasure.

The Empire of Songhai

The Kingdom of Songhai rose up from the ashes of the Mali Empire. Its leader, Sonni Ali, was a great military commander. According to legend, his capture of the city of Djenne in 1477 took seven years, seven months and seven days! His army also conquered the cities of Gao and Timbuktu, and Niani, the capital of Mali. However, as Ali did not fully embrace Islam, he did not have the popular support that his successor, Askiya Muhammad, was able to achieve.

Askiya Muhammad

Askiya Muhammad (1493–1528) was able to use his religious beliefs to great advantage, signing deals with the Arab merchants across the Sahara to secure good trading relationships and using his Imams (priests) to get support for his government in the mosques. He also used

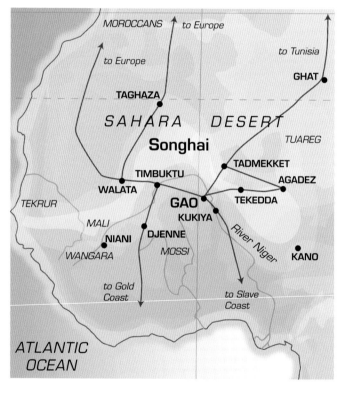

▲ The Kingdom of Songhai spread rapidly during Askiya Muhammad's rule to become an empire.

▲ The tomb of Askiya Muhammad is a World Heritage Site. It can be found in Gao, Mali.

his army to increase the size of the Songhai Empire to the north. They took control of the important salt mines in the Sahara, and attacked the Hausa kingdoms in the east. The Songhai Empire was so large by the 1520s that it was bigger than the whole of Europe.

However, Askiya Muhammad was not only interested in military matters – he was also a man of learning. During his reign, thousands of schools were opened, the University of Sankore Mosque in Timbuktu was developed and thousands of books were published. Muslim scholars taught Arabic, law, mathematics and astronomy. and students came from around the world to study.

▶ *The Sankore Mosque still stands today in Timbuktu. Highly skilled scholars produced manuscripts such as the one shown below (inset).*

Invasion

The end of the Songhai Empire came about as a result of an invasion from the north. In 1591, the Sultan of Morocco sent his army (led by a Spanish mercenary) across the Sahara to capture the gold mines of Songhai. The Sultan had been able to buy cannon and other weapons from the English Queen, Elizabeth I. As a result, his forces were too strong for the Songhai army, which was easily defeated. The last of the great West African empires had come to an end, and the influence of Europeans in Africa was on the rise.

Did you know?

A writer called Leo Africanus, who wrote a book called *A History and Description of Africa,* claimed that, "more profit is made from the book trade (in Songhai) than from any other line of business." This is pretty amazing when you think about how much gold there still was in West Africa, as well as the incredibly valuable salt and copper trade.

A rough guide to Timbuktu

IN DEPTH

Background for your visit to 16th-century Timbuktu

Many people think that Timbuktu is not a real place, but it is! According to legend the name comes from the words 'tin', which means watering place, and 'buktu', the name of a woman who fed her animals there. It is one of the most important places in Songhai, because so many people go to trade there, and it is the centre of trade for gold. There are many mosques, schools and libraries to visit, and students from across Africa live there.

If you visit Timbuktu in 1518, you can be there for the Silver Jubilee (25 years) anniversary of Emperor Askiya Muhammad.

Map of Mali today

ALGERIA

Salt mines of Taoudenni

Araouane

Timbuktu

MAURITANIA

River Niger

to Djenne

to Gao

Getting there

Timbuktu is on the River Niger, in the southern part of the Sahara desert. This is a great chance for you to take part in a camel trek, where you can go from the great trading city of Djenne to Timbuktu. If you go from Gao, you can take a canoe along the River Niger. Be warned though, the journey from the Mediterranean to Timbuktu could take you two months!

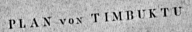

▶ *A 14th-century plan of Timbuktu.*

PLAN von TIMBUKTU

¼ Geographische (deütsche) Meile

1. Dschama el Kebira (die grosse Moschee, im Bau, begonnen vone Sultan Mille im J. 1325)
2. Moschee von Sankore
3. Moschee Sidi Jahia
4. Platz genannt Timbutu bottema
5. Haus des Scheich el Bakay
6. Marktplatz
7. Haus wo Dr Barth wohnte
8. Abèras, die Vorstädte

Getting around

Be careful, Timbuktu is not the easiest place to get around. The streets are dusty and the gates of the city are closed at night, so you need to make sure you have a place to stay. You also need to be careful about fire – in c.1512, half of the city was burnt down in less than five hours!

◀ You must visit a market on your trip to Timbuktu.

Where to stay

You may be able to find a *funduq*, or guest house, if they haven't been taken up by the merchants who normally stay there. A funduq normally has plenty of rooms, and even places for your camels to stay. You will also be able to keep your belongings safe, as the merchants normally store their goods there too.

Things to see and do

✪ Plans are being drawn up for a great University at Sankore, where thousands of students will be able to study law, literature, maths and medicine.

✪ You should also check out the markets, especially if you want to pick up some clothes. Apparently the women are so beautifully dressed that they are covered in jewels. The market is so wealthy that the goods you buy are served to you on plates of gold.

✪ According to Leo Africanus, the houses are huts made of clay with thatched roofs. In the centre of the city is a temple built of stone and mortar, and a large palace where the king lives.

Djinguerebere Mosque is one of the must-see sights.

The Kingdom of Benin

OVERVIEW

Around the same time as the Songhai Empire was expanding, the smaller Kingdom of Benin to the east was also growing under the leadership of Oba (King) Ewuare the Great (1440–73). The capital, Benin City, had a huge defensive wall and moat around it. The wall was the biggest ever built anywhere in the world, even bigger than the Great Wall of China!

Benin City

A Dutch visitor to Benin City in 1668 described it in the following way:

▲ *This illustration of Benin City is from c. 1686. The figure on horseback is the Oba.*

"The town … is protected by a wall three metres high … with several gates … has 30 very straight and broad streets, everyone of them about 36 metres wide … the houses have roofs made of palm or banana leaves … the walls are made of red clay, very well erected, and they can make and keep them as shiny and smooth by washing and rubbing … and they are like mirrors."

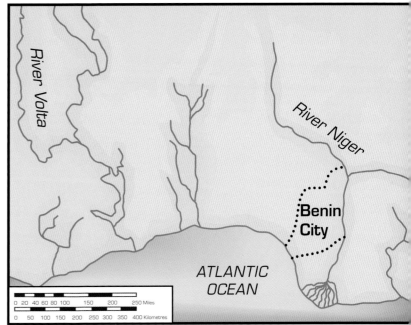

▲ This map shows the vast size of Benin City and its wall – an area now in modern-day Nigeria.

Trade

Benin's wealth was based on the trade carried out by its merchants. They traded materials such as ivory, pepper and cotton across the Sahara to the north. However, where Benin differed significantly from the other West African empires was in its trade with Europeans. The Portuguese bought dyed cotton cloth, leopard skins and palm oil, as well as slaves, in return for guns and other manufactured goods. Guns and ammunition gave the Benin military a huge advantage over their local rivals.

The Benin bronzes

The craftsmen and women of Benin had fantastic skills, particularly in metalwork. The Benin bronzes (which are actually made from brass) are hundreds of different objects showing everyday life. They include casts of heads of religious leaders, such as the Oba, as well as Portuguese traders, alongside different animals and fish. When the British army invaded Benin in 1897, over 200 of the Benin bronzes were removed and taken to the British Museum in London. Many have still not been returned to Benin.

▼ This Benin bronze shows a prince on horseback wearing chainmail – a type of armour introduced by the Portuguese in the 15th century.

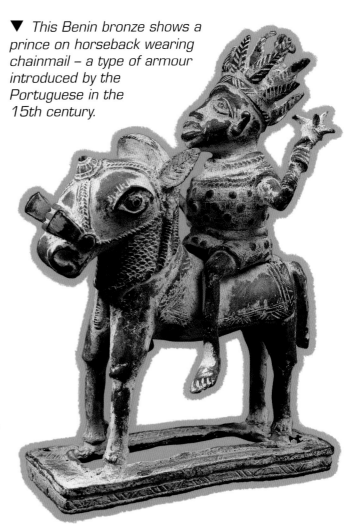

Living in Benin

Although there are not many written records about the Kingdom of Benin, one of the best sources that tell us about life in Benin comes from Olaudah Equiano. He was captured as a slave in the 1750s and taken to the West Indies. Equiano wrote about his experiences in his autobiography, *The Interesting Narrative of Olaudah Equiano, or Gustavus Vassa, the African*, which was published in 1789.

The following extracts are Equiano's own words about growing up in Benin:

Equiano describes the house that he lived in;

"Our day-houses are left open at the sides; but those in which we sleep are always covered, and plastered in the inside, with a composition mixed with cow dung, to keep off the different insects, which annoy us during the night. The walls and floors also of these are generally covered with mats. Our beds consist of a platform, raised about a metre from the ground, on which are laid skins, and different parts of a tree called plantain."

▲ *This image of Olaudah Equiano was drawn by Daniel Orme in 1789.*

The clothes that the men and women wore were similar;

"It generally consists of a long piece of calico, or muslin (cloth), wrapped loosely round the body ... This is usually dyed blue, which is our favourite colour. It is extracted from a berry, and is brighter and richer than any I have seen in Europe. Besides this, our women ... wear golden ornaments."

▲ *You can see different clothing in this woodcarving from the Kingdom of Benin. The four bound figures are thought to be prisoners.*

The food that was eaten was varied, but mainly consisted of vegetables;

"Our vegetables are mostly plantains, yams, beans and Indian corn ... Our pineapples are about the size of the largest sugar-loaf, and finely flavoured. We have also spices of different kinds, particularly pepper; and a variety of delicious fruits."

▲ *Ears of Indian corn – now called variegated maize.*

There were also important customs that were carried out;

"The head of the family usually eats alone; his wives and slaves have also their separate tables. Before we taste food we always wash our hands: indeed our cleanliness on all occasions is extreme. After washing, libation (a religious ceremony) is made by pouring out a small portion of the drink on the floor ... for the spirits of departed relations."

▼ *These women from modern-day West Africa are dancing and wearing traditional clothes.*

And on many important occasions there was a lot to celebrate;

"We are a nation of dancers, musicians and poets. Thus every great event, such as a triumphant return from battle, or other cause of public rejoicing is celebrated in public dances, which are accompanied with songs and music suited to the occasion."

Great Zimbabwe

OVERVIEW

The development of large-scale communities was not confined to East and West Africa. There were also fascinating developments taking place in different parts of the continent. One of the greatest monuments in southern Africa is Great Zimbabwe; a huge settlement of stone walls and soapstone carvings built around 1300 CE by people of the Shona tribe. These buildings are so important that Zimbabwe, the country that they are in, was eventually named after them.

◀ These are part of the ruins of Great Zimbabwe.

▼ This illustration shows the complete extent of the ruins, with the wall running round the outside in an oval shape.

When Vicente Pegado, a Portuguese soldier, visited Great Zimbabwe in 1531, he described what he saw:

"Among the gold mines of the inland plains between the Limpopo and Zambezi rivers, there is a fortress built of stones of marvellous size, and there appears to be no mortar joining them ... there is a tower more than 22 metres high."

The fact that these walls were 'dry' – in other words built without cement holding them together – meant that the people who built them must have been very skilful. The granite would have been carved carefully, so that the stones fitted neatly on top of each other. There were also eight soapstone carvings of birds around the walls, which had a mix of human and bird features.

Did you know?

It seems that the walls of Great Zimbabwe were not necessarily for defensive purposes, but more likely to show the importance of the people living there. It is likely that no more than 300 people actually lived in Great Zimbabwe itself. There were also many smaller zimbabwes dotted around the region, where up to 10,000 people would have lived.

▼ *This is one of the soapstone figures that helped link Great Zimbabwe to the Shona tribe.*

▲ *One of the soapstone birds of Great Zimbabwe. This one has a damaged face.*

Trade

Based on the findings of archaeologists, Great Zimbabwe was also an important trading area with the Middle East, China and India. Pottery from Persia (Iran) and China, and coins from Arabia, have been discovered there. When the Portuguese came to East Africa they wanted to take control of these valuable trading routes, which is why they came to places such as Great Zimbabwe.

The end of Great Zimbabwe

No one really knows why people suddenly stopped living in Great Zimbabwe, but by the 15th century it had been abandoned. Some historians have suggested that it may have been too unhealthy to live there (the bite of a Tsetse fly causes deadly sleeping sickness), or it could have been caused by drought or the decline in the gold trade.

Who built Great Zimbabwe?

IN DEPTH

One of the great things about being a historian is that you can be a bit of a detective. In the same way that a detective needs clues to solve a crime, historians need clues or evidence to help find out about the past. However, what happens if the clues are not telling us the whole truth? The story of who built Great Zimbabwe is an important lesson. Over time, different people have used the evidence to tell a different stories. Today, few people dispute that it was built by the Shona people around 1300 CE, but this was not always the case.

Story 1 – the first great white lie

The first European archaeologist to visit Great Zimbabwe was a German man, called Carl Mauch, in 1871. This was a time when many people in Europe had racist ideas about Africa. When he saw the impressive buildings he couldn't believe they were built by Africans. So instead, he said that these buildings must have been erected by King Soloman and the Queen of Sheba (two Biblical figures).

Story 2 – the second great white lie

When the British took control of the area where Great Zimbabwe was (it was called Rhodesia from 1895 after Cecil Rhodes, the Prime Minister of the Cape Colony), they asked an archaeologist to investigate the ruins. Richard Hall wrote a book called *The Ancient Ruins of Rhodesia*, in which he argued that Great Zimbabwe had been built by "more civilised races" than the Africans. Hall even went so far as to remove about two metres of archaeological material, which meant that all the evidence was lost for future generations. He even justified this by saying that he was, "removing the filth ... of Kaffir (a racist word for Black Africans) occupation."

▲ *Carl Mauch helped spread the great white lie.*

▲ Gertrude Caton-Thompson was one of the first people to identify that Great Zimbabwe was built by Africans.

Story 3 – the truth is out

Finally, in 1931, another British archaeologist, Gertrude Caton-Thompson, was able to prove once and for all that Great Zimbabwe was built by Africans. She was able to use the remaining evidence from different artefacts and the houses that survived, and compare it with the history that she had learned from the Shona people to prove that Great Zimbabwe was built by Africans.

Story 4 – still hiding the truth

However, even after this evidence was made available, the government of Rhodesia denied it. Paul Williams was an archaeologist at

▶ A modern African sculptor with a soapstone carving. Soapstone carvings are still produced by the Shona people today.

Great Zimbabwe and he was told by his managers not to mention anything about Africans building the site:

"I was told that the museum service was in a difficult situation, that the government was pressurising them to withhold the correct information ... Once a member of the Museum Board of Trustees threatened me with losing my job if I said publicly that blacks had built [Great] Zimbabwe."

Now, however, every visitor to Great Zimbabwe is able to find out the truth about the largest historic structure south of the Sahara.

These stories show us different interpretations of the past, and how difficult it can be for historians to work out what really happened. That is why historians need to be good detectives, to use the evidence that is available to them to reach their own conclusions about the past.

The Europeans arrive

There have been many instances of Africans coming into contact with Europeans throughout history. The Greeks, for example, learnt a lot about medicine from the ancient Egyptians. However, the main reason for this contact was for trade: Africa provided many raw materials that were used across Europe, including gold, ivory, spices and pepper.

One of the most terrible consequences of this contact was the development of the Transatlantic Slave Trade; where Europeans enslaved millions of Africans to work in the 'New World' of the Americas. You can read more about the transatlantic slave trade in *Black History: Africa and the Slave Trade*.

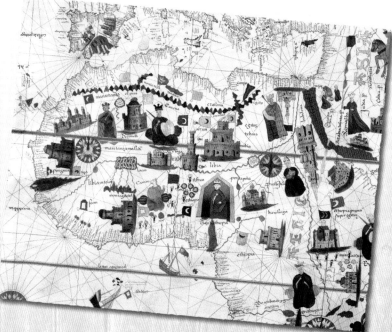

▲ *This map was drawn by the Portuguese explorer, Juan de la Cosa c.1500.*

Trading posts

The first modern Europeans to make contact with Africa were the Portuguese in the 1440s, when ships belonging to Prince Henry 'the Navigator' landed in West Africa. Within 30 years, trading posts were set up along the Gold Coast (modern day Ghana) and the fort at Elmina was established. Elmina soon became notorious as one of the most significant slave trading 'factories' where hundreds of thousands of enslaved Africans passed through on their way across the Atlantic.

The explorers

Other European countries also wanted to profit from their relationships with Africa, especially France and Britain. The French were particularly interested in the North African countries which bordered the Mediterranean Sea. Meanwhile, the British hoped to extend their influence from 'the Cape to Cairo', which meant all the way from South Africa at the southern tip of Africa to Egypt at the top. However, for this to happen it would mean getting access to the central part, or the 'heart' of Africa. This had always proven difficult as most of the rivers in

▲ *British explorer John Speke (left) is shown presenting rhinoceros heads as a gift.*

▼ *The Conference of Berlin (1884–1885) carved up Africa between different European nations.*

Africa were not easily navigable by boat. Many different explorers set out to find routes into the interior. The most famous were John Speke, who discovered the source of the River Nile in 1858 (which he named Lake Victoria after Queen Victoria of England), and David Livingstone, who became the first European to cross Africa from coast to coast in 1856.

The Scramble for Africa

By the late 19th century, the European involvement in Africa was coming to its peak. In 1884, at the Conference of Berlin, the leaders of Europe agreed to divide up Africa between themselves. The Africans were to have no say in the matter.

African resistance

There were many examples of Africans resisting the colonisation of their land by the European imperialists. Here are just two examples: Queen Nzingha from Angola, who fought against the Portuguese; and Yaa Asantewaa, the woman who led the resistance in Asanteland (now Ghana) against the British.

Case Study 1: Queen Nzingha (1583–1663)

Nzingha Mbande was born in 1583 into the ruling family of the Mbundu tribe, in the part of south-west Africa now known as Angola. By the time she became queen

▲ This print of Queen Nzingha is by Pierre Duflos (1742–1816), who painted African portraits.

in 1624, her people were involved in a series of conflicts with the Portuguese who had come to Angola to trade in goods, including enslaved Africans.

According to a famous story, two years before she became queen, Nzingha went to meet the Portuguese Governor, Correia de Sousa, to discuss a treaty between the two nations in 1622. De Sousa did not offer the Queen a seat, so instead her attendants rolled out a carpet for her and one of them went down on all fours so that she could sit on him and not be humiliated by sitting on the floor.

The Portuguese did not honour their part of the treaty to reduce their amount of slave trafficking, and so Queen Nzingha started the first of a series of wars against them. She even went as far as making an alliance with the Dutch against the Portuguese, and ended up fighting against them for nearly 30 years. One of the most important things that she did was to declare that her land would be 'free', which meant that there would be no slavery there.

Case Study 2:
Yaa Asantewaa (1840–21)

Yaa Asantewaa was the Queen Mother of the Asante tribe. The British exiled the King of Asante, Prempeh I, in 1896. Shortly afterwards, the British Governor of the Gold Coast demanded that the Asante hand over their 'Golden Stool'. The stool was one of the most important symbols of the Asante people and losing it would have been a further humiliation. At a meeting of the tribal leaders, Yaa Asantewaa stood up and said:

"Now I see that some of you fear to go forward to fight for our king … chiefs would not sit down to see their king to be taken away without firing a shot. Is it true that the bravery of Asante is no more? I cannot believe it. It cannot be! I must say this: if you, the men of Asante, will not go forward, then we will. We, the women, will. I shall call upon my fellow women. We will fight the white men. We will fight till the last of us falls in the battlefields."

▲ *This early photograph shows Asante officials with the Golden Stool (centre).*

Yaa Asantewaa led the Asante rebellion in 1900 which lasted for two years until she was captured and exiled. Finally, the Asante had been defeated and the British were able to control the Gold Coast.

▼ *This image, by Denis Dighton, shows the 'defeat' of the Asante at the hands of rifle and sword-wielding British forces in 1824.*

A timeline of African Empires

c.3400 BCE   The Kingdom of Ta-Seti (sometimes called Kush)

c.3000   The First Dynasty of Egyptian pharaohs

c.2500   The pyramids at Giza are built

c.300 CE   The Kingdom of Ghana is founded

c.700   Islam sweeps across North Africa

c.800 – c.1000   The trans-Saharan trade routes open up

1076   Tenkamenin, Emperor of Ghana, fights against Muslim invaders

c.1200   The Kingdom of Mali is founded

1235   Sundiate Keita becomes Mansa (Emperor) of Mali

c.1300   The Shona people start to build Great Zimbabwe

1312   Mansa Musa rules Mali

c.1440   Portugal starts trading with West Africa, including the first slaves

Oba Ewuare becomes the leader of Benin. Work starts on the walls and moat around Benin City

1468   Sunni Ali forms the Songhai Empire

1481   Elmina, a fort which was used for holding enslaved Africans, is built by the Portuguese

1493   Askiya Muhammad becomes ruler of Songhai

1591   An invasion from Morocco leads to the breakup of the Songhai Empire

1622   Queen Nzingha attacks the Portuguese in Angola

1652   Dutch settlers take over Cape Colony in South Africa

1660   The Royal African Company is set up by the British to trade slaves from Africa

1660–1833   The height of the Transatlantic Slave Trade, an estimated 30 million Africans are taken to the Americas

1789   Olaudah Equiano publishes his autobiography, *An Interesting Narrative...*, to campaign against the slave trade

1856   David Livingstone crosses Africa from east to west

1858   John Speke reaches the source of the River Nile

1884   The Conference of Berlin divides Africa up between the European powers, starting the 'Scramble for Africa'

1900   The Asanti wars begin, led by Yaa Asantewaa, fighting against British control of the Gold Coast (Ghana)

Key:

- The formation of African Empires
- Trade
- Resistance
- Explorers

Websites and Bibliography

Websites

www.ancientegypt.co.uk
From the British Museum, this website has a huge amount of material about ancient Egypt ranging from mummification to Egyptian gods.

www.nationalarchives.gov.uk/pathways /blackhistory/africa_caribbean/west_ africa.htm
Overview of the West African Empires before European influence.

www.ghanaweb.com/GhanaHomePage /history/ancient_ghana.php
This website has an overview of the history of Ghana from ancient times until modern day. You can also find about Yaa Asantewaa here (**www.ghanaweb.com/GhanaHomePage /people/pop-up.php?ID=175**)

www.metmuseum.org/toah/hd/ wsem/hd_wsem.htm
This website, from the Museum of Metropolitan Art in New York, has a series of overviews of the West African empires including Ghana, Mali and Songhai. You can also find out about Great Zimbabwe here. (**www.metmuseum.org/toah/hd/zimb/ hd_zimb.htm**)

http://www.muslimmuseum.org/ 1005/sankore-university
Information about the University of Sankore, Timbuktu.

http://countrystudies.us/ghana/ 6.htm
From the US Library of Congress, this website has a lot of information about the early European contact with West Africa and Ghana in particular.

http://en.wikipedia.org/wiki/Nzinga_ of_Ndongo_and_Matamba
Information about Queen Nzingha who fought against the Portuguese in the 1620s.

http://web.cocc.edu/cagatucci/ classes/hum211/timelines/htimeline 2.htm
A detailed timeline of African history from the 1st to the 15th century.

Bibliography

Boyd H, *African History for Beginners*, For Beginners LLC, 1994

Haywood J, *West African Kingdoms*, Harcourt Education, 2008

Ibazebo I, *Africa Exploring History* , Belitha Press, 2003

Oliver R and Atmore A, *Medieval Africa*, Cambridge University Press, 2001

Parker J and Rathbone R, *African History A Very Short Introduction*, OUP, 2007

Van Sertima I (Ed), *Great Black Leaders: Ancient and Modern*, Journal of African Civilisations, 1988

Equiano, O, *The Interesting Narrative and Other Writings*, Penguin Classics, 2003

Glossary

Allah Muslim name for God.

Alliance A political friendship or agreement between countries or tribes.

Anthropology The study of human beings and their way of life.

Archaeology The study of artefacts, inscriptions, monuments and other remains that tell us about the past.

Barter A form of trade where one person exchanges his goods for another's.

BCE (Before the Common Era) A system of numbering dates to show that the number refers to a date before the current era.

CE (Common Era) A system of numbering dates to show that they are from the current era.

Chainmail A type of protective armour made up of many linked rings of metal.

Christianity The religion based on the teachings of Jesus Christ.

Civilisation A particular society at a particular time and place.

Colonisation When one country/nation takes over another it is known as colonisation.

Culture The arts, beliefs and traditions of a particular society.

Dynasty A sequence of rulers from the same family. For example, the First Dynasty of ancient Egypt was believed to have started around 3100 BCE and lasted until 2890 BCE.

Empire When one country/nation rules over one or more other countries/nations. For example, Mali ruled over an area which was as large as Western Europe. The ruler of an empire is called an emperor.

Exile To force someone to leave their country and not allow them to return.

Explorers A person who travels to a foreign country to learn about it. European explorers are often described as discovering a country, meaning the brought it to the attention of people back home.

Exports Goods sold to foreign countries.

Far East A term used to refer to the countries east of India and including Thailand, China, Korea, Malaysia, Indonesia and Japan.

First Dynasty of Egypt A succession of rulers from the same family who were the first to hold power in ancient Egypt.

Funduq A place where travellers and merchants could stay in cities in the Songhai Empire such as Timbuktu.

Hadj/Hajj One of the most important elements of Islam is the pilgrimage to Mecca, the birthplace of the Prophet Muhammad (*peace be upon him*), known as the Hajj. Muslims are supposed to go on the Hajj at least once in their lifetimes.

Henna A plant used to make a red-brown dye.

Hieroglyphics The picture writing of the ancient Egyptians.

Islam The religion of the followers of the Prophet Muhammad (*peace be upon him*). They are called Muslims.

Ivory The tusk of an elephant used to make objects, piano keys, knife handles etc.

Kingdom An area of land which is ruled over by a king, for example the Kingdom of Benin in West Africa.

Mercenary A soldier paid to fight for a country other than his or her own.

Missionary A person sent to spread his or her religion to people who don't follow that religion.

Mosque The place of worship for Muslims.

Oba The ruler of Benin was called the Oba.

Pharaoh The name given to the political and religious leader in ancient Egypt.

Pilgrimage The journey of a religious person, undertaken as an act of worship.

Primary source A source, such as an eyewitness, which comes from the time of the event that is described.

Proverb A popular saying with words of advice or warning.

Scramble for Africa
At the Berlin Conference (1884–1885), European countries agreed to divide the continent of Africa between themselves. This started what became known as 'the Scramble for Africa'.

Soapstone A type of rock used for carving.

Trade The buying and selling of goods. In West Africa some of the most valuable goods to be traded were salt and gold.

Trade routes The routes that merchants took to buy and sell their goods. For example in North Africa the trade routes went across the Sahara desert.

World Heritage Site A site of great importance that is on UNESCO's list of World Heritage Sites.

Index

These are the lists of contents for the titles in *Black History*: